I'VE STILL GOT IT!

Other Crankshaft Books from Andrews and McMeel

... And One Slice with Anchovies!
Crankshaft

I'VE STILL GOT IT!

A **CRANKSHAFT**® collection
by Tom Batiuk and Chuck Ayers

Andrews and McMeel
A Universal Press Syndicate Company
Kansas City

AND FINALLY, EVEN THE SEATS ON THIS BUS ARE STATE·OF·THE·ART. THEY'RE ALL TRIPLE TEFLON COATED....

SO THERE'S ABSOLUTELY NO POSSIBLE WAY TO GET COMFORTABLE IN THEM!

AND I FEEL THIS NEW SCHOOL BUS THAT THE BOARD JUST PURCHASED, SHOULD GO TO ED CRANKSHAFT....

FOR BACKING UP SO MUCH TRAFFIC BEHIND HIS BUS LAST YEAR...

THAT THE STATE HAS JUST AUTHORIZED A NEW BYPASS TO BE BUILT AROUND HIS BUS ROUTE!

I THINK THE ELECTRIC HAIR DRYER IS A REALLY GREAT INVENTION!

DUSTING HAS NEVER BEEN EASIER!

I'LL HAVE TO GIVE HER CREDIT....

SHE'S NO QUITTER!

THE LITTLE JOHNSON GIRL IS STILL HANGING IN BACK THERE CHASING AFTER THE BUS!

IT'S FUNNY, BUT I COULD TELL FROM THE VERY FIRST TIME I SET EYES ON HER...

THAT SHE WAS GOING TO BE A TOUGH ONE!

IT WAS PROBABLY THE TATTOO...

IT'S BEEN SUGGESTED THAT SINCE SO MANY OF OUR KIDS MISS THE BUS EACH DAY....

INSTEAD OF ALL OF US DRIVING THEM TO SCHOOL SEPARATELY....

WE SHOULD FORM A 'CRANKSHAFT CARPOOL'....

OUR SCHOOL BUS DRIVER, MR. CRANKSHAFT, IS MAKING ALL OF US MOTHERS CRAZY....

AND SO...WE'VE ESTABLISHED THIS SUPPORT GROUP TO HELP US DEAL WITH OUR FEELINGS.

THE HECK WITH THAT! LET'S DEAL WITH CRANKSHAFT!!

YEAH! RIGHT!

NOW LADIES...

I SAY WE MOTHERS HAVE GOT TO BAND TOGETHER AND DO SOMETHING ABOUT OUR SCHOOL BUS DRIVER, MR. CRANKSHAFT!

SHE'S RIGHT!

MY LITTLE BOY, ROBBIE, MISSED THE BUS SO MANY TIMES LAST YEAR, HE HAD TO REPEAT THE THIRD GRADE!

...AND AS THE SCHOOL BUS PULLED AWAY, JOANNE WAS LEFT STANDING THERE IN THE MIDDLE OF THE STREET IN HER NIGHTIE, HOLDING A SMURF LUNCHBOX, CURSING AT THE TOP OF HER LUNGS!

I MAKE A MOTION THAT WE IMMEDIATELY DEVISE A PLAN TO DEAL WITH CRANKSHAFT...

AND THAT WE PAY FOR JOANNE'S BAIL!

AND THEN THERE'S POOR EVONNE WILSON...

SHE SPENT SO MUCH TIME RUNNING AFTER CRANKSHAFT'S BUS LAST YEAR...

THAT SHE HAD TO SPEND THE SUMMER AT THE BETTY FORD CLINIC TO KICK HER ADDICTION TO EXHAUST FUMES!

OKAY, THEN IT IS AGREED THAT THE 'CRANKSHAFT CARPOOL' WILL AUTHORIZE THE FUNDS TO HIRE THE GENTLEMAN IN QUESTION.

DOES ANYONE KNOW HOW THIS 'EQUALIZER' PERSON CAN BE CONTACTED?

HIS AD IS RIGHT HERE IN THE CLASSIFIEDS..

BATIUK & AYERS

SO, WHO DO YOU THINK IS GOING TO WIN.... BUSH OR DUKAKIS?

APRIL 89

MORT HAS DEFINITELY GOT TO WORK UP SOME NEW SMALL TALK!

EVERYBODY'S HAIR HAS ITS OWN UNUSUAL CHALLENGE FOR A BARBER!

OH YEAH?

MORT'S BARBER SHOP

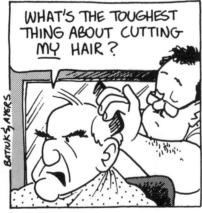

WHAT'S THE TOUGHEST THING ABOUT CUTTING MY HAIR?

BATIUK & AYERS

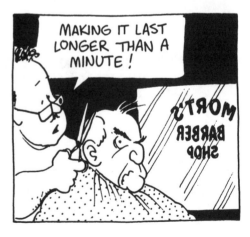

MAKING IT LAST LONGER THAN A MINUTE!

MORT'S BARBER SHOP

DID IT!! I FINISHED YOUR RETURN AND I STILL HAVE A HALF HOUR TO GET IT IN THE MAIL BEFORE THE MIDNIGHT DEADLINE!!

I'M JUST GLAD THAT NONE OF MY FELLOW ACCOUNTANTS CAN SEE ME DOING THIS!!

OUR 'I MISSED IT' NEWS CAMERAS ARE LIVE IN FRONT OF THE POST OFFICE WHERE LATE FILERS ARE RUSHING TO BEAT THAT MIDNIGHT DEADLINE....

JEFF...? DAD...?

I QUIT! I'VE LOST THE EDGE! I CAN'T DRIVE A SCHOOL BUS ANYMORE!

WHAT'S THAT PICTURE ON YOUR DESK!? KIDS!!

AAAAAAAAAAAAAA!!!

BUS DRIVER BURNOUT ISN'T PRETTY!

CRANKSHAFT, AS YOU KNOW, EVERY YEAR WE SEND OUR BEST BUS DRIVER TO A SPECIAL TOP SECRET TRAINING SCHOOL.

I WAS GOING TO SEND BILL, BUT HE CRACKED UP ON ME....SO IT LOOKS LIKE THIS YEAR, YOU'RE THE ONE WHO'LL BE GOING TO....

TOP RUN

17

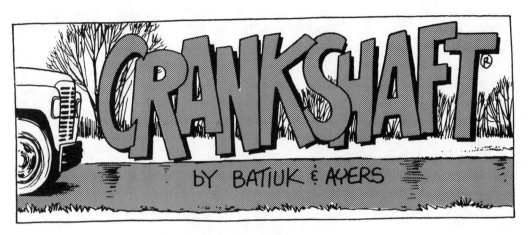

21

NO DOUBT ABOUT IT, GRACE...

YOU REALLY KNOW HOW TO COOK!

HOW ABOUT A SECOND HELPING?

I'M SORRY, ED... I DIDN'T REALIZE YOUR LEGS WERE BROKEN.

OH, I GET IT... NO PROBLEM, YOU CAN GET IT WHEN YOU'RE FINISHED.

THAT'S STILL NOT RIGHT, IS IT?

DID YOU HEAR THE NEWS? THE MOTHERS ON ED'S ROUTE HAVE HIRED THE 'MASKED MOTHER' TO CATCH HIS BUS!

I'VE ALWAYS HEARD THAT THE 'MASKED MOTHER'S' FEE WAS PRETTY STEEP!

THAT PROBABLY EXPLAINS ALL THE GARAGE SALES ON MY ROUTE THIS PAST WEEK!

THE 'MASKED MOTHER' WILL NEVER CATCH OL' CRANKSHAFT! HE'S THE TOP GUN!

THAT'S WHAT WE ALL LIKE TO THINK, SON....

BUT SOONER OR LATER, WE'RE ALL GOING TO RUN INTO A MOTHER WHO'S JUST A LITTLE BIT QUICKER....

THEY'RE SAYING THE 'MASKED MOTHER' IS GOING THROUGH A SPECIAL PROGRAM JUST TO GET READY TO TAKE ON CRANKSHAFT!

NO KIDDING....

COME ON! **PUSH!** YOU'LL NEVER CATCH HIM IF YOU'RE NOT STRONG ENOUGH TO CARRY YOUR SPEED THROUGH THE HILLS!

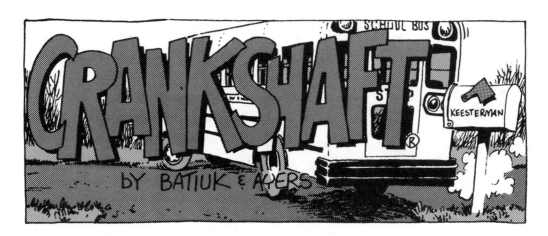

29

32

33

I WON'T BE NEEDING YOU ANYMORE TODAY, ED....

BUT I'LL EXPECT YOU TOMORROW AT EIGHT A.M. SHARP!

ARRRRGGGHHHH!

IT DRIVES HIM CRAZY!

SIT DOWN AND SHUT UP!

THE NEXT ONE WHO GETS UP OUT OF HIS SEAT IS GOING TO BE WALKING HOME!

OKAY...THE NEXT AWARD TO BE GIVEN OUT FOR TONIGHT'S BUS DRIVERS' AWARD BANQUET IS....

AS YOU KNOW, ED CRANKSHAFT HIT THE CENTURY MARK THIS SPRING, WHEN HE FLATTENED MILO KEESTERMAN'S MAIL-BOX FOR THE ONE HUNDREDTH TIME IN HIS CAREER....

AND IN RECOGNITION OF THAT, THE NATIONAL ORGANIZATION IS PROUD TO HONOR ED....

WITH THIS YEAR'S "BRONZE MAILBOX" AWARD....

THIS YEAR'S "OUTSTANDING BUS DRIVER OF THE YEAR" AWARD GOES TO ED CRANKSHAFT....

WHO, ONCE AGAIN, LEFT MORE KIDS OUT STANDING FOR THE BUS THAN ANY OTHER DRIVER!

44

47

HEY! WHAT'S GOING ON!!?
OUR CAR ISN'T COMING BACK!

OH, NO! IT'S
GOING OUT INTO
THE STREET!

SCREECH!!!

CRUNCH

I DON'T KNOW WHAT IT IS...

BUT I JUST DON'T SEEM TO HAVE THE ENERGY I USED TO!

FACE IT, CRANKSHAFT... YOU'RE NOT GETTING ANY YOUNGER!

IF YOU'RE NOT CAREFUL... **YOU'RE** NOT GOING TO GET ANY **OLDER** !

63

GO **AHEAD**!

DO IT **YOUR** WAY!!

NOBODY AROUND HERE EVER PAYS ANY ATTENTION TO WHAT **I** HAVE TO SAY !!

EH..., I SUPPOSE I SHOULDN'T HAVE BARKED AT PAMELA THE WAY I DID....

WHEN AM I EVER GOING TO LEARN?

IT'S NOT FAIR...I'M JUST NOT MATURE ENOUGH TO BE AS OLD AS I AM!

CRANKSHAFT

BY BATIUK & AYERS

WHAT'RE YOU DOIN', GRAMPS?

I'M GOING TO FIRE UP THE OLD BARBECUE!

OH BOY!

PAY ATTENTION, MAX, AND YOU CAN LEARN THE "CRANKSHAFT NEVER FAIL METHOD" FOR STARTING A BARBECUE!

SQUIRT! SQUIRT! SQUIRT!

SQUIRT! SQUIRT! SQUIRT!

THERE... SEE HOW THE CHARCOAL IS STARTING TO BOB AROUND?

I'LL GO SEE IF WE STILL HAVE RED ADAIR'S PHONE NUMBER!

AND I'LL ALWAYS REMEMBER HOW YOU'D DRIVE WITH YOUR ONE ARM RESTING ON THE WINDOW AND YOUR ICE CREAM CONE IN THE OTHER...

CHRISSY AND I WOULD BE SITTING IN THE BACK SEAT WITH OUR BARE FEET UPON THE BACK OF THE FRONT SEAT.

YOU'D YELL AT US TO PUT THEM DOWN, BUT WE'D ONLY SLIDE THEM DOWN FAR ENOUGH SO YOU COULDN'T SEE OUR TOES STICKING UP.

YOU WHAT?

WHAT'S WITH MOM?

ED?

DON'T LOOK AT ME...YOU KNEW SHE WAS CRAZY WHEN YOU MARRIED HER!

STEPPING IN AT THE PLATE WITH TWO OUT IN THE EIGHTH...

WHERE'S YOUR DAD OFF TO NOW?

COUNTY FAIR

HE'S HEADED FOR THE PRODUCE BARNS.

AS LONG AS HE WAS COMING TO THE FAIR, HE FIGURED HE'D ENTER HIS KILLER BEE HONEY!

73

HAPPY ANNIVERSARY, ED!

IT WAS EXACTLY ONE YEAR AGO TODAY THAT YOU STARTED TO LEARN TO READ!

I SUPPOSE THIS ISN'T THE BEST TIME TO TELL YOU THAT I'VE DECIDED TO QUIT, IS IT?

ED, YOU CAN'T **QUIT** YOUR READING CLASS!! YOU'RE JUST DISCOURAGED BECAUSE YOU'VE REACHED A PLATEAU AND YOU FEEL YOU'RE NOT MAKING ANY PROGRESS.

BUT THAT'S VERY COMMON WITH PEOPLE WHO ARE LEARNING TO READ. IT'S NOT AN EASY THING TO DO.

I NEVER PROMISED YOU A PROSE GARDEN!

CUTE!

SEE? YOU **HAVE** MADE PROGRESS!

ALL THESE YEARS YOU COULD ONLY LOOK AT THE PICTURES ON THE COMICS PAGE... BUT YOU COULD NEVER UNDERSTAND ANY OF THE STRIPS!

NOW YOU'RE ABLE TO SIT HERE AND READ 'FUNKY WINKERBEAN'!

MAYBE SO... BUT I STILL DON'T GET IT...

74

77

MISSY, WHAT'S WRONG?

:SOB!: AND THEN THE TEACHERS AT SCHOOL ARE GOING TO LOCK US IN CAGES, FEED US BEETLES AND NEVER LET US COME HOME AGAIN!

HONEY, THAT'S RIDICULOUS!

WHO ON EARTH PUT ALL OF THESE RIDICULOUS NOTIONS INTO YOUR HEAD?

CRANKSHAFT! I WANT A WORD WITH YOU!!

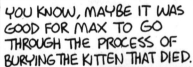

YOU KNOW, MAYBE IT WAS GOOD FOR MAX TO GO THROUGH THE PROCESS OF BURYING THE KITTEN THAT DIED.

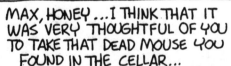

YEAH, A LITTLE **TOO** GOOD...

ANYBODY GOT ANYTHING THEY NEED BURIED?

MAX, HONEY...I THINK THAT IT WAS VERY THOUGHTFUL OF YOU TO TAKE THAT DEAD MOUSE YOU FOUND IN THE CELLAR...

AND BURY IT IN GRANDPA'S SHOEBOX.

BUT THE NEXT TIME...

BE SURE TO TAKE THE NEW SHOES OUT OF THE BOX!

GRAMPS...TELL ME AGAIN ABOUT THE INNING WHEN YOU STRUCK OUT THE TOP OF THE TIGERS' LINEUP!

HERE'S THE PITCH...

MAX, DON'T BOTHER YOUR GRANDFATHER...HE MUST'VE TOLD THAT STORY A HUNDRED...

WELL, IT WAS THE SUMMER OF 1940 AND THE TIGERS HAD COME DOWN TO PLAY AN EXHIBITION GAME AGAINST THE TOLEDO MUD HENS....

STRIKE TWO!

IT WAS THE SUMMER OF 1940 AND THE TIGERS HAD COME DOWN TO PLAY AN EXHIBITION GAME AGAINST THE TOLEDO MUD HENS....

HE SETS HE PITCHES...

IT WAS THE THIRD INNING AND I WAS GETTING SET TO FACE THE TOP OF THE TIGER ORDER WHEN MY CATCHER, DUSTY BOTTOMS, CAME OUT TO THE MOUND TO TALK OVER OUR STRATEGY...

BALL ONE!

I JUST WANTED TO WISH YOU GOOD LUCK!

MY CATCHER AND I WENT OVER THE HITTERS...

HANK GREENBERG, CHARLIE GEHRINGER AND RUDY YORK ARE DUE UP!

WHAT WE'RE LOOKIN' AT HERE IS TWO POTENTIAL HALL OF FAMERS AND A GUY WHO'S ALREADY GOT OVER A HUNDRED RBIs THIS SEASON!

WHAT SHOULD I DO?

FAKE AN INJURY!

86

CRANKSHAFT

BY BATIUK & AYERS

AND NOW IT'S TIME FOR 'IN MY OPINION'....

A CHANCE FOR OUR VIEWERS TO SAY WHAT'S ON THEIR MINDS!

in my opinion

I'M ED CRANKSHAFT AND I'M A SCHOOL BUS DRIVER.

in my opinion

SCHOOLS ARE BACK IN SESSION...SO IF YOU'RE OUT AND ABOUT, BE EXTRA ALERT IN SCHOOL ZONES...

in my opinion

NEWS

BECAUSE THOSE HIGH SCHOOL KIDS DRIVE LIKE GOL DANGED MANIACS!!!

UH, THANK YOU, MR. CRANKSHAFT...

AND IF YOU VALUE YOUR LIFE...DON'T GO NEAR THE BURGER BARN LOT AFTER NINE O'CLOCK!!

BATIUK & AYERS

HERE COMES THE LITTLE JOHNSON GIRL BARRELING DOWN THE DRIVEWAY.

IT'S AMAZING HOW SHE CAN RUN THAT FAST WITHOUT SPILLING ANY OF THE CUPCAKES ON THAT TRAY SHE'S CARRYING!

THAT LITTLE JOHNSON GIRL IS BACK THERE RUNNING AFTER THE BUS WITH THAT TRAY OF CUPCAKES FOR HER HALLOWEEN PARTY.

HOW SHE'S ABLE TO MANAGE THAT **AND** THE FRENCH HORN IS BEYOND ME!

THE LITTLE JOHNSON GIRL HASN'T GIVEN UP.

SHE'S STILL CHASING THE BUS WITH THAT TRAY OF HALLOWEEN CUPCAKES.

ALTHOUGH SHE HAS SLOWED SOME SINCE THAT PLASTIC WRAP FLEW OFF THE TRAY AND STUCK TO HER GLASSES!

96

99

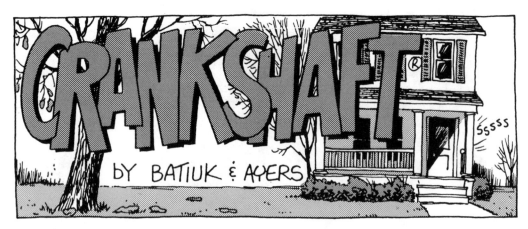

HERE! I GOT SOME CRANBERRY SAUCE.

OH, THAT'S REALLY SWEET, DAD, BUT I WAS GOING TO MAKE MY OWN CRANBERRY SAUCE FROM THIS RECIPE IN THIS MAGAZINE.

NAW, LET'S HAVE THE OLD FASHIONED KIND... FROM A CAN!

NO KIDDING! THE LITTLE JOHNSON GIRL GAVE YOU SOMETHING FOR THANKSGIVING?!

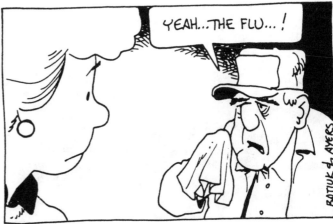

YEAH...THE FLU...!

SINCE GRANDPA ISN'T FEELING TOO WELL, LET'S TAKE HIS THANKSGIVING DINNER UP TO HIM!

GREAT!

♪ OVER THE DRIVEWAY AND UP THE STAIRS...TO GRANDFATHER'S HOUSE WE GO.... ♪ ♫

107

I'LL GO OVER YOUR REPORT CAREFULLY...

AND WE'LL ELIMINATE THAT VIOLATION!

HOW DID THE O.S.H.A. INSPECTION OF OUR BUS GARAGE GO?

NOT TOO BAD....

WE ONLY HAD ONE VIOLATION....

OSHA
VIOLATION REPORT

LENA'S COFFEE!

GOOD NEWS, ED...THE POLICE THINK THEY'VE FOUND YOUR BUS AND THEY'D LIKE YOU TO GO IDENTIFY IT!

EH, ALL RIGHT....

A PLANE TICKET?

IT'S IN THE PARKING LOT AT DISNEY WORLD!

THAT'S MY BUS ALL RIGHT!

WE PICKED THEM UP AFTER WE GOT A REPORT OF AN ENTIRE SCHOOL BUS MOONING THE PASSING LANE ON THE EXPRESSWAY!

WHAT ARE THEY DOING?

DUSTING THE WINDOWS FOR BUTT PRINTS!

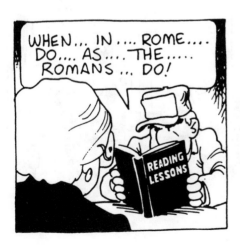

WHEN... IN.... ROME.... DO.... AS.... THE..... ROMANS ... DO!

THAT WAS VERY GOOD, ED! DO YOU HAVE ANY QUESTIONS?

YEAH... WHAT DO THE ROMANS DO?

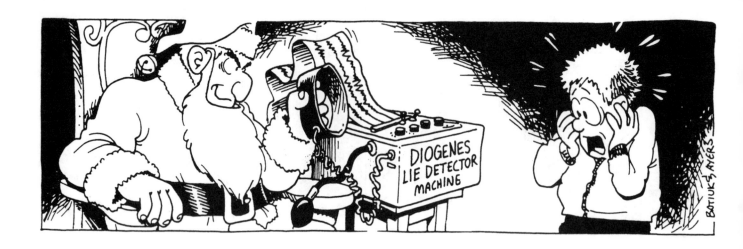

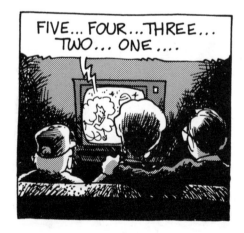